Hi Louise,
Thank you for [...] ...k.
I look forward [...] !!
Love me [...]

Lost in Mind:
Found at Heart

Lost in Mind; Found at Heart

Published by The Conrad Press Ltd. in the United Kingdom 2021

Tel: +44(0)1227 472 874
www.theconradpress.com
info@theconradpress.com

ISBN 978-1-914913-54-9

Copyright © Melanie Haagman, 2021

Printed and bound in Great Britain by Clays Ltd, Elcograf S.p.A

Typesetting and Cover Design by The Book Typesetters
www.thebooktypesetters.com

The Conrad Press logo was designed by Maria Priestley.

Lost in Mind: Found at Heart

Melanie Haagman

Author's dedication

I would like to dedicate this book to my followers who I've gained through sharing my work on *Girl on The Edge Poetry* on Facebook.

You have been such a huge support and inspiration behind everything. When I first started sharing poems, I never imagined it would lead to such strong, loyal bonds that have been created.

The support you provided me with during the writing of *Lexical Lockdown*, was incredible. Without it, I wouldn't have had the courage and motivation to create these books.

Thank you for your kind words, your loyalty and your ongoing support. I'm glad we have helped each other to know that even in the most difficult of times, we are not alone, and the power of words will continue to unite us and offer us comfort in even our darkest days.

Preface

Lost in Mind; Found at Heart really did write itself. Every time I feel a strong emotion, whether it be a negative or a positive one, I find nothing more therapeutic and satisfying than writing a poem about it and of course they have always got to rhyme!

Poetry for me is an innate coping mechanism to deal with whatever life throws at me. I do my best to try and write honestly and always aim to end with an uplifting line. This book reflects that no matter how hard things get, when we are truthful and transparent with our emotions, we can make meaningful connections with others who will in turn help us to get through. As well as learning how to get back up when we fall and realising that this is how we learn, develop, and grow.

It has never been more important to speak out about mental health and the similar struggles that we are facing. I hope that these poems can help others to know that they aren't alone with their feelings.

This book is divided into sub-sections to quickly help you find the perfect poem to get you through the day. Whether you need advice, a little injection of humour, a poem about feelings, down-days, or even friendship!

I hope that you can laugh, cry, smile, relate to and most importantly enjoy this book.

You can follow me on my Facebook Poetry Page: https://www.facebook.com/Girlontheedge90/

Melanie Haagman, November 2021

Contents

Feelings

Feelings

Feelings are confusing,
They come and go all day,
Some of us express them
Some keep them locked away.
Feelings can take over,
They're tricky to explain,
And the ones we try to hide,
Are those of hurt and pain.
But feelings are uniting,
They help us feel connected,
Which is why it's dangerous
When they are neglected.
Feelings take us by surprise,
Not matching expectations,
Like when we feel so upset,
At times of celebrations.
However you are feeling,
Know it's absolutely fine,
And don't be fooled that others
Feel happy all the time…
So, sharing how you feel,
Is such an important thing to do
And the care from other people
Will help you to get through…

Speak out

There once lived a man who had so much to give,
He had so many reasons to continue to live.
But the world was cruel and the mind unkind,
And internal peace was a challenge to find.
So he battled alone, feared what others may say,
And continued to hide his true sadness away.
Faking a smile was success he achieved,
When he said he was fine, it was always believed.
He wanted to speak but the fear was too strong,
So he battled in silence like nothing was wrong.
No desire to eat, his whole being felt numb,
Even he didn't recognise the man he'd become.
Soon breathing became a draining chore,
He was so tired but didn't sleep anymore.
This stayed the same for what felt like forever,
Where life seemed like a hopeless endeavour…
Until one day he picked up the phone,
And discovered right then that he wasn't alone.
Reassured that he was far from weak,
He broke his silence and started to speak.
And he gained the support that was required,
Now to live, not to die is what he desired.
And through sharing his story and his pain,
He aims to help others to do the same.

You were here

You were here and you affected me
In a way no one else could ever do
You were here and you inspired me,
And I've been changed by you.
I will try not to feel pain and sorrow,
You were here and that should be enough,
For I was lucky to have known you
Yet at times things still feel tough.
You were here and you taught me things,
That I never would have learnt,
You were here for many years,
And then suddenly you weren't.
You were here and you encouraged me
To strive to be whatever I desired,
You were here and then you weren't
For your guidance had expired.
You were here and that's what matters,
And your influence won't die,
Which means that when I lost you,
I never said goodbye.

Who are you?

Is it the choices that you make
That determine who you are?
Or the status of your postcode,
Or the price of your new car?
Or is it the acts of kindness
That altruistic trait.
Or your never-ending patience
And acceptance of your fate?
Is it through your friends,
Your family, your morals
Or that you don't hold grudges
Despite your frequent quarrels.
Is it that deep inside
You're ultimately kind
And a soul like yours
Is difficult to find?
What is it that defines you,
What marks will you leave on Earth,
Or are you getting tired
Of trying to prove your worth?
Because all that really matters
Does not amount to much,
Except for the hearts of others
That you have truly touched.

My mum

I'm so good at hiding it,
All the pain I feel,
I compartmentalise it all,
As if it isn't real.
I want to speak about you badly,
But my mouth doesn't comply,
I wish I could explain it,
But I don't even know why…
I think about you all the time,
And what could have been,
If you hadn't had to leave us,
When I was just thirteen…
But I hope that you are happy,
With the woman I've become,
And there's not a day goes by
Where I don't miss you, Mum…

(In memory of my mum)

Equality

In life everything changes,
Except the mindsets of some,
Yes, we've come a long way
But there's much more to be done.
Imagine a world with justice,
And unconditional love,
Where we don't have to pray
To the heavens up above.
Because here, every day,
While we breathe and we live,
We don't have to forget
We don't have to forgive.
All the chaos and hate
Would exist no longer,
And when humans unite,
They only grow stronger.
Imagine a world of equality,
Where difference is embraced,
And the prejudices of today
Are no longer faced.
Imagine a world where there's peace,
Acceptance, and no need to define
Who you are or where you're from
Let's mark this moment in time.

When we can hug again

I've missed the embrace,
Of a hug and a squeeze,
Which makes me feel
So much more at ease.
I didn't realise how deprived
I'd feel without a hug,
And I've concluded
It's the best human drug.
This automatic greeting
That connects the human race,
Has been taken away,
To preserve our 'safe space'.
My arms fail to rise,
As it's been so long,
Because I've been conditioned
To feel that it's wrong.
Many months have gone by,
And there are more to endure,
We all miss a cuddle
That's one thing for sure.
But let's hope that soon
we can squeeze, hug and kiss
All of our loved ones
That we desperately miss.

Behind the words

It's not so much the words
Or the way they are combined
But the passion of the writer
And the power they've assigned.
It's not so much the poem,
But the way that it's perceived,
All the emotion that's behind it
And the message that's received.
It's not so much the rhythm,
Or the emphasis or beat,
But the connections that are found
Without the need to meet.
We all have similar thoughts,
Fears, experiences and more,
So, the ability to relate to all
Is what my writing's for…

Compassion

Compassion is crucial,
Compassion is key,
It brings to light,
What you need to see
Self-indulgence
Isn't self-care,
And that gets mixed up.
Almost everywhere.
But so much is subjective,
Opinions are utterly rife,
So hard to know what's right
In this multifaceted life.
But as long as there's compassion
In the people all around me,
I know that it's just a mindset
When it comes to being free.

Emotional intelligence

Emotional intelligence,
Picking up on social cues,
Knowing it's impossible
To put yourself in others' shoes
Knowing when not to speak
For silence is a skill,
Having the awareness
To foresee how others feel.
But to demonstrate all this
You must master who you are
And once you get to know yourself
My God, you will go far.
Emotional intelligence
Doesn't get the prestige it deserves,
And many people lack it,
From what I have observed.
This skill can be learned,
It's not something that's innate,
Let's master our emotional education
Before it is too late.

Autumn

The crisp autumnal air
That I love to inhale,
And the crunch of flattened leaves
Left behind me as a trail.
The temperature, refreshing,
As it hits my pale skin,
And I feel a sense of happiness
From somewhere deep within.
Autumn's my favourite season,
The clothes are just the best,
The boots and the jackets,
But no need to wear a vest.
Halloween and fireworks,
Toffee apples on a stick,
The days are dark so early,
And they fly by in a tick.
Sitting by a fire, in a warm and toasty pub,
Making soups and winter stews,
Yes, I love the summer sun,
But it's autumn I would choose.

The fear of failure

The fear of failing at anything
Is something we must defeat,
Failure is a springboard
To successes we're going to meet.
Without the rejections
There's no time for reflections
To change, to grow, to adapt,
Not to make us feel trapped…
But to send us surges of motivation,
That we desperately need
To bounce back, be resilient
And learn how to succeed.
Confront the fear head on,
It's not personal at all,
Because if you want to climb high,
You've got to learn how to fall.
Embrace the experience,
You know how to improve,
Don't be paralysed with fear,
But keep on the move…
When we fail we make progress
It's all part of the process.
Compassion is created,
Even though you are frustrated.
Find peace with failure,
It's a part of life for most,
And those who don't experience it
Are the ones who may boast.

But they lack the compassion,
They've not had the same ride,
And from their success
They won't gain the same pride.

My favourite things

The smell of coffee roasting,
The sun shining bright,
The notion of acceptance
That it's going to be alright.
The hard work paying off,
Seeing friends succeed,
And the true joy you acquire
From a satisfying read.
Learning from mistakes,
And truly laughing hard,
Being the authentic you
And letting down your guard.
Dancing in the kitchen,
And running for no reason,
Dressing for autumn,
Because that's the best season.
Not having to explain yourself,
Just communicating with a look,
And know that you made your point,
An expression is all it took.
Playing tennis and doing well,
When the ball is in full swing,
Knowing that in this time,
The brain won't fear a thing.
Writing all the poetry,
Offloading inner chat,
These are some of my favourite things
And I'll leave it at that.

Rejecting morals

To live a life in battle,
Isn't something I could bear,
To hate the world around me,
And the people everywhere.
To reject the norms and values,
Instilled in us to date,
Would leave to never-ending pain
And new levels of hate…
Seduced by your own sadness,
Segregated and alone,
Feeling lost and lonely,
Unhappy with your home.
Who wants to fight each day?
There's so much joy to seek,
More laugher and happiness
That can enrich your week.
Wrong and right aren't black or white
In between there's so much more,
So pack away your weapons,
We don't need another war.

Apathy

I'd rather feel too deeply
About things great and small
Than lack any emotion
And feel nothing at all…
Hate's not the opposite of love
It's apathy instead,
And I really hope this trait
Doesn't multiply and spread.
Successful communication
Won't be able to take place,
Barriers in relationships
Will be the constant case.
Apathy can be temporary
Though a dangerous path to tread,
You may feel such emptiness
Now your feelings have fled.
No sense of impending doom,
Or any elation to share,
A brain once on fire,
Is now silent and bare.
Acknowledgment is crucial,
The start to being freed,
And finding motivation
To get exactly what you need.
In a world with endless potential
There's so much good to feel,
So get inside the car of life
And strongly steer the wheel.

Friendship

Friendship

It matters not how long it's been,
Since you last have spoken,
You know full well this doesn't mean
Your friendship is now broken.
For best friends are the long-haul ones,
Where no grudges form and stay,
And they understand that sometimes
Life gets in the way.
They listen and they give advice
But don't judge if they're ignored,
And you know that if you needed them
They'd be right at your front door.
Friends find joy in your success,
No jealousy is shown,
And if you're blessed to find these friends
You'll never feel alone.

Life

What do you want from life?
To be heard and understood.
What do you want to do?
To be interpreted as good.
How do you want to be?
Calm, happy and true,
Not question every action,
Approach each day brand new.
Where do you see yourself?
Anywhere I feel at home,
What do you wish the most?
To never feel alone.
Are you happy right now?
It varies day to day,
Do you have any regrets?
I do but cannot say.
What do you deem as strength?
To be self-assured and bold,
How long do you want to live?
Until I'm very old.
Can money buy you happiness?
No, but it stops a lot of stress,
Unless you are free soul,
I'm not, I must confess.
What wisdom have you gained?
To know things always improve,
When frozen with grief and pain,
You'll soon learn how to move.

What do you fear the most?
To be misunderstood,
To lack the tact I need,
To make the point I should.
When do you write the most?
When strong emotions pour,
The ones you cannot keep inside,
Because they really roar.
Where is your favourite place?
In my dreams, the peace they bring,
And when I'm with the ones I love,
Who give me everything…

Human

There's no malice in my actions
Though they aren't always right
I'm no coward when I walk away
I just don't want to fight.
I'm not ignorant when I don't understand
I'm not closed off to learn
And sometimes I keep walking straight
And forget I need to turn.
Sometimes my words may hurt
But that is not what I intend
And sometimes I know that I
Could be a better friend.
Sometimes we do things
And regret them straight away
But we are all just human
And we're learning every day.

A hard time to be a friend

We're all a bit depressed right now,
It cannot be denied,
Whether this is shared openly,
Or is something that we hide.
We are trying hard to help ourselves,
To steer toward the light,
And others are going backwards
They've a harder war to fight.
It's never been more tough to be a friend,
You can't even look them in the eye,
You don't want to answer, 'How are you?'
Without the urge to cry.
So how do you support your friends,
When you're struggling yourself,
In this time of significant strain
Upon our mental health.
A question, I can't answer,
I don't know what is best,
But picking up the phone's a start,
And you'll figure out the rest.

(Written during the Pandemic of 2020)

Perception

Is it an opinion
The truth or just a lie…
Did I misunderstand
And forget to question why…
Did you not get the humour
Of the darkest, driest kind,
Because I found it funny,
Or was it just my twisted mind?
Did I not notice the emotion?
That came before you spoke,
Do you think that I'm asleep
And I'm far from being woke.
I thought that your behaviour,
Came from a place that's insecure,
So, I didn't react back to you,
Like I might have done before.
Do I think that all this kindness
Came truly from your heart?
Or was there an ulterior motive
Lying dormant from the start?
Do you come from deep hardship?
The pain you have is palpable,
Or was it all embellished
And you took me for a fool?
Perception is opinion,
Something that's based on thought,
And I am wired from experience
My perception is self-taught.

It alters every single day,
With each passing blunder,
But will it inhibit me all my life,
Is something that I wonder…

I'm here

I hear it in your voice,
I see it in your eyes,
The outpourings of grief,
You're unable to disguise.
The strength that you possess,
Many could not endure,
And collectively it's made you
Even stronger than before.
Although these cruel events,
Have stolen way too much,
You've always got back up.
Providing others with a crutch,
And when you're down and lonely,
Exacerbated by these days,
Know that I'm not far away,
And here for you always…

Deep connections

The trauma, the turmoil,
The pain and the fear,
The hurt and the heartbreak
That won't disappear.
They bring us together,
Or have the adverse effect,
But can be the reason
We deeply connect.
We grow from the hard times,
And better becomes best,
We were warned about life
And it being a test.
We can't compare pain,
It's relative as can be,
But speaking and sharing
Can set some of it free.
So open yourself up,
As wide as you can,
Living in solitude
Wasn't part of the plan.
Use what you've been through,
From a meaningful existence,
The power behind it
Will sure go the distance.

Listening

I want to understand you,
What has led you to be here.
I want to hear your story,
What you crave and what you fear.
I want to know your choices,
What you've accepted and declined,
I want to know your future,
And what you hope to find.
I want to know about your influences,
Through the life that you now live,
I want to know if you hold a grudge,
Or can you easily forgive?
I want to learn your mind-set,
The core values that you hold,
And how you keep so grounded,
With the beliefs that you've been told.
I want to show you respect and trust,
To be open and to share,
And I will cast no judgement,
By showing you, I care.

Down Days

The dark days

Today I feel lonely, aloof and unheard,
Living in a world that can be so absurd
Today I feel mopey though I don't want to be,
And I'm really not liking very much about me.
Today I feel angry, powerless and sad,
Focussing only on all that is bad.
Today I feel like just hiding away,
And there isn't much left I want to say.
Today I feel and I don't want to feel,
I want to block out all that is real.
Today I feel I've lost my head,
And I just want to stay in bed.
Today I feel this negative way,
But tomorrow, I know, I'll be okay.

Hard to be happy

Sometimes it's hard to be happy,
To smile, to laugh and spread hope,
Sometimes it's fine to be miserable,
To sit on the sofa and mope.
Sometimes it's hard to sleep,
You can't drift off and chill,
You need a little helping hand,
From that herbal sleeping pill.
Sometimes it's hard to listen,
Your mind is just too loud,
You want to be all by yourself
Not in a chatty crowd.
Sometimes it's hard to cook,
You've had a tricky day,
So if you want *Deliveroo*
It's really quite okay.
Sometimes it's hard to get up,
You cannot leave your bed,
So stop beating yourself up
And stay right there instead.
Sometimes routine can halt,
Consistency needs a break,
No pressure or guilt needed,
Just a deep breath – try to take.

The keyboard warriors

As you sit behind your screen,
You feel safe, you're not seen.
You write words that cut deep,
How can you even get to sleep?
I feel for you all the same
You must be in some sort of pain,
To fill your time with things unkind,
I hope soon solace you can find.
But know your words have a consequence
That could go beyond causing offence.
Maybe you have faced some hate
And think you must retaliate.
But revenge is not best served cold
Despite what you've always been told.
Don't press send, take a break
And think about what's at stake.
A life, a person who's had enough,
Dealing with this hidden stuff.
Don't be the cause of so much pain,
There's more to life that you can gain.

Anxiety

If I could take away the anxiety,
The complete over-reaction,
The way the thoughts escalate
As they keep gaining traction…
The inability to help them stop,
No words you can hear,
And the thoughts are a phobia,
Eliciting genuine fear.
Deep inside a brain, hidden away.
With a fire spreading at speed,
And talking about it makes it worse
It's hard to know what you need.
Anxiety is crippling, but your body moves,
It comes in staggering blasts,
The feeling cannot be maintained,
No matter how long it lasts.
No one deserves to live this way,
Spiralling as they ebb and flow,
Triggers work their magic,
And the anxiety begins to grow.
So if you witness this in someone,
It's tangible and real,
And you wish you could cure it all
For it's far from the ideal.

The fear

Expectations and desire,
What does all this require?
We are young and then we're not,
Our aspirations forgot…
Are we stuck in a rut?
Too scared to let go,
We've got to take risks,
Or we'll never really know!
Is this path that I've taken,
All I'm truly meant to be?
Is this part of the world,
All I'm ever going to see?
All these questions fill my mind,
None of which I can solve,
But I want to progress,
I want my life to evolve…
But I remain stationary,
Static and still,
I'm held back by the fear,
Consuming all that I feel.

The guilt

The guilt, the guilt, the guilt,
That consumes me from within,
It knows exactly how to dwell
On every mundane thing.
The things I should have done,
And the words I should have said,
They loop and loop repeatedly,
Exploding in my head.
The failures that have led me
To where I am today,
Should only be celebrated
For the crucial role they play.
Though not an easy thing to do,
Changing patterns we've created,
And to now think differently
Is rather complicated.
But acknowledgement's a start,
And next we must rewire
All the negative thought patterns
And new outlooks we'll acquire.
Forgive and let go of the past,
The should haves and regret,
You'll feel lighter than ever
Not emotionally in debt!

Humour

Rhyming loyalty

What you hear is what you get
I love a simple rhyme,
After all, I think it's clear
They've stood the test of time.
Poetry is interpretive
To no rules must one adhere,
Some poetry is simple
And some is not quite clear.
I love a metaphor and simile,
But some take it to an extreme,
And I have trouble understanding
Just what the verses mean.
I like relatable poetry,
Of the humorous vein
Like Pam Ayres the genius
Who doesn't hurt my brain.
This stems from some workshops
Where I have read aloud,
And been the only one who rhymes
Among a larger crowd.
It appears a rhyme is old school,
Not a modern thing to do,
But to my rhyming musings
I will always stand by you.

The toilet roll holder

I bought my Grandma a present,
Designed to make her laugh
It was a toilet roll holder
In the form of a giraffe.
The toilet rolls go down the neck
And sit next to the loo,
But when it arrived at Grandma's
She was unsure what to do.
Clearly confused by the gift,
And I could tell by her voice,
That she didn't like it much
And I had made the wrong choice.
I heard nothing more about it
Until I next went round,
And when walking in the living room,
I was amused by what I found.
The toilet roll holder
On the mantelpiece it sat,
And had taken pride of place
In her beautifully furnished flat.
Maybe it wasn't obvious,
The purpose it was for,
But I couldn't speak to tell her
I was laughing on the floor.

Designer clothes

Labels and designer clothes
Are a guilty pleasure of mine
I'm all for Tommy Hilfiger
And a bit of Calvin Klein!
I rarely pay full price
As they are always so high
So when there is a sale
It's the greatest time to buy.
There's nothing like a bargain,
Picking up a brilliant deal
Nothing beats the satisfaction
Of knowing it's a steal.
There's nothing snobby about it,
It's the quality, so durable,
That causes my addiction to be
Utterly incurable.

Morning television

Since I changed my working hours,
I find myself engrossed
In morning television
Whilst munching on some toast.
So entertaining in many ways,
I enjoy them in a row,
But *This Morning* with Phil and Holly
Is my all-time favourite show.
There is just one small problem,
The competitions draw me in,
And I justify each entry
With belief that I will win.
They show 'ordinary people'
Whose lives were turned around,
When they texted to that number
That cost them just two pounds.
The problem is… I've not won yet,
But the possibility I'll seize,
Though I really could've bought that car
With all my entry fees.

The healing power of laughter

The laughter that's wholesome
Comes straight from inside,
The laughter that's real
You're unable to hide.
Nothing compares to laughter
When your stomach is in pain,
Even if you don't feel it,
It helps you to stay sane.
The laughter where your cheeks ache
Is what I truly treasure,
You can't overdose on laughter
There is an infinite measure.
Smiling makes others smile,
Mirror neurons are so real,
And laughter has an effect
On how deeply you feel.
Reducing stress and even pain,
Immunity's increased,
Laughter is infectious
And endorphins are released.
Laughing is the best medicine,
In this life that can be tough
And if you can hold onto it,
It just might be enough!

Brand new

Today is the day…
For a brand new healthy me,
I'm going to quit the sugar
And take up the herbal tea.
I'm going to go veggie
No more dairy I'll consume,
And the running that I paused
I will urgently resume.
I've had enough regretting
The bad choices I have made,
I hate that it takes half an hour
For my jean indent to fade!
It's just been so boring lately,
And with not much we can do,
I've been eating for leisure
And I can't say that it's not true.
But today this stops entirely,
And food is not my friend,
Now I have to go and dash,
I have a soup to blend.

Reality TV

Immersing yourself in the life of others,
Helps you to forget about your own
And this is my favourite thing to do
In the evening, when at home.
These people are outrageous
You know it can't be real,
They're unbelievably dramatic
With expressing how they feel.
The Real Housewives of Beverly Hills
I watch, though I can't relate
With their diamonds and their butlers
Taking care of their estate!
They live lives of luxury
Indulging in the best
But money doesn't bring happiness
They have problems like the rest.
I really shouldn't love it
And should limit what I see
But I just can't get enough
Of this reality TV.

Social skills in lockdown

I feel I've lost my social skills,
Since they were tossed aside
And now when I'm in company
I'm frankly terrified.
I talk too much, or not enough
I just can't get it right,
And things come out rudely
When I mean to be polite.
For too long now I've been inside,
Not engaging in this skill
I never was the best at it
And now it's gone downhill.
I overshared my life story,
With someone I barely knew,
And didn't tone it down at all
Like I would normally do.
I feel more opinionated
Than I ever have before,
But now I must remember
To leave them at the door.
So now that we can socialise
Of course, in safer mode,
I'm hoping it'll get easier
To recall the social code.

(Written during the Pandemic of 2020)

Grandma's TV

Grandma's TV was pretty old,
The quality and style,
She'd had it for fifteen years,
More than a little while...
But to her it was still new,
She didn't desire an upgrade,
Despite the fuzzy picture,
She demanded that it stayed.
But now the days are long,
With limitations unlike before,
And if she had a Smart TV,
She could access so much more.
So I bit the bullet and bought her one,
It's the least that she deserves,
And sometimes it's company
That these electricals can serve.
Her reaction wasn't excitement,
But sheer terror and alarm,
It was as if I told her something
That would cause her major harm.
I knew once it was installed,
Watching TV wouldn't be a chore,
As she could explore Netflix,
Like she's never done before.
And when it was all working,
Her fears dwindled away,
She said she'd sell the old one,
Like she'd find someone to pay!

But it would just be used for scraps,
This she couldn't accept at all
So we installed in her bedroom
And now she thinks it looks quite cool.
So let's hope she masters Netflix,
And maybe even Prime,
Knowing the need for an upgrade,
Had truly reached its time.

Grandma's shopping

'Here's my list, my lovely girl,'
Her tone all soft and sweet,
So I make my way to Tesco,
For my Grandma has to eat!
I carefully select her items,
I'm sure to pick the best,
Anything that's incorrect
Just won't pass the test.
I check the trolley twice,
For her shop must be exact,
I take it to the tills
And ensure it's neatly packed!
I take it to her immediately,
As I'm met with gratitude,
But as she unloads the bags,
There's a change in her attitude!
'I didn't ask for two pints of milk,
And I really hate this bread,
I asked for Granny Smiths,
How on earth were you misled?'
I hope this is the last I'll hear,
Of her dissatisfied tone,
But come 3 days later,
When we're speaking on the phone…
'I'm just eating those apples…
The ones you wrongly bought…

They're spongey and revolting...'
And I can't suppress the thought....

DO YOUR OWN SHOPPING!

The driving range

I can't say I'm a golfer
But I love the driving range
And when I get a club in hand
I feel a massive change.
Something overcomes me,
An anger deep within,
And I funnel this emotion
To produce the wildest swing.
When you hear the ting
And the ball takes flight
You feel such satisfaction
Because you've hit it right.
The problem is afterwards,
The blisters on my hand,
The jarring of my body
And I can barely stand.
I vow next time I'll calm it down,
But I know I never will,
I love whacking golf balls
Across a green or up a hill!

The bin bag

I bought some scented big bags,
Because you've got to find some ways
To add a little excitement
Into these rather boring days…
When I opened up the packet,
Pulled the bin bag out to see,
I was extremely shocked,
These weren't any use to me!
The bin bag was minuscule,
Like something I'd never seen,
The size of a sandwich bag,
It was really quite obscene!
A bin bag for a dolls house,
Who owns a bin so small?
But later on, I looked again,
And deemed myself a fool.
It wasn't open fully,
It was folded up quite tight,
And when I shook it hard enough
The size turned out just right.
With not much entertainment
Or funny things to make you smile,
This stupid occurrence
Had me laughing for a while.
So I had to take to paper,
This situation I went through,
Because at the moment,
There's not much else to do!

To the tormentor in my hand

I know you are important,
A purpose you sure serve,
But I give you way more time,
Than you definitely deserve.
I hold you in my hand,
As I stare into your screen,
Revisiting the utter crap
That I've already seen.
Aimlessly unlocking,
Muscle memory takes control
As I mindlessly continue
With the never-ending scroll.
Mainly I see adverts,
They listen to when I speak,
And I compare my average body
To a perfect toned physique.
But still I take you with me,
On walks and when I run,
And get irritated when I struggle
To see you in the sun.
But now a detox is needed,
Not from my poetry page,
But unless it's really important,
I'm going to disengage.
Because I'm too reliant,
On this drug we call a phone,
So next time I go out,
I'm going on my own!

Anyone for coffee?

Multi-tasking is vital,
It's built in and innate,
And productivity can occur
At a much faster rate.
But when you're not on form,
And focus can be tricky,
The situations you get into
Can be rather sticky.
The coffee-making task,
Done mindlessly and quick,
May be the very reason
That makes you rather sick.
The coffee granule tin,
That I grabbed without a care,
Was actually the Bisto,
But I was unaware.
The granules went in the mug,
The milk and sweetener too,
And then the boiling water
(I still didn't have a clue).
Until I took the first sip,
A shock it was indeed,
A glass of meaty Bisto,
Isn't something that you need.
So make sure your pots are separate
Don't make the same mistake,
I think I'll forget the coffee
And just have that slice of cake.

Quad bikes

I've never been a thrill-seeker,
I get my kicks elsewhere,
I won't ride the rollercoaster,
At the park or at the fair…
I see risks in everything
Worst outcomes flood my brain,
So I try and stick to safety,
Living life in the slow lane.
Life is scary enough,
Adrenaline's never far away,
It avalanches through my blood
At least ten times every day.
So when I had to quad bike,
I tried the best I could,
And in such an anxious mindset,
I wasn't very good…
Turn and go couldn't be achieved,
At the same time for me
And I went in the wrong direction,
To the other three…
They took to it like ducks to water,
Relaxed and chilled they were,
As I clutched on tightly
Waiting for injury to occur.
I didn't make it past the small field,
The woods were next to see,
With tight turns and extreme tracks,
That truly weren't for me.

So I turned around abruptly,
With shaky arms, I pulled the key,
And jumped back into my car,
Some things aren't meant to be!

Advice

Step outside your silence

I see you in the background,
Standing out by blending in,
I hear you when you're silent,
And patience is wearing thin…
I feel all of your frustration,
It oozes from your soul,
I sense that you have lost a lot
And it's left a gaping hole.
I can taste your disappointment,
Life's not gone the way you'd hoped,
But you've hidden it so well
Bad habits helped you cope.
I can see you in the background,
Standing out by blending in,
I can hear your thoughts quite loudly
Reverberating from within.
I can see what you're disguising,
From the words you never say,
I can see you've built a barrier,
To keep the world at bay.
But step outside your silence,
You've so much more to give,
You were put here for a reason
So don't forget to live.

Superpower

'What is your superpower?'
Asked the little boy,
As he clutched on tightly
To his Spiderman toy.
'To be kind always,'
Is what his teacher said,
But the young boy laughed
And shook his tiny head.
'That's not a superpower,'
He replied with a certain tone,
'Yes it is, my little friend,
You'll realise when you're grown.'
This stuck with him forever,
Stayed cemented in his brain,
And now when his children ask
His answer is the same...

You are enough

(A reverse poem)

You are not enough today
Don't ever say that
You are trying your hardest
You can always do better
Stop thinking that
You will get there
Without punishing yourself
You have to find the power to succeed
You are not loved
You are not important and
You must stop thinking that
You are doing your best

(Now read bottom up)

The news

So many of us rely on
The media for truth
And blindly accept a lot
With not much need for proof.
So we live a life of confusion
From one day to the next,
Where information changes
Leaving us to feel vexed.
It doesn't just change a little bit,
It changes to extreme,
And often trying to scare us
Remains its constant theme.
I don't mean everything we read
Is not based on some fact,
I just wish headlines were written
With quite a lot more tact.
In a nation with anxiety,
Why escalate and feed?
Because further fear and panic
Isn't something that we need.
We want to solve the problems,
But we have to be productive.
We need the way the news is shared
To change how it's conducted.

Reading

Absorbed in someone else's life,
Temporary escape and relief,
Relating to others' pain,
Their highs, their lows, their grief.
In these moments you're gone,
You are lost within the page,
The emotions are palpable
From elation to rage.
There is no better feeling
Than immersing yourself in fiction
The words may be the same
But not the readers' depiction.
Reading is such a luxury
But in this busy life – rejected,
So, don't allow yours
To be literary neglected!

Addiction

(A reverse poem)

I need to eat chocolate every day
Don't try to convince me that
I don't need chocolate
I am too weak to refuse it
I will always succumb to its cravings and
Don't ever say
I can resist it
Chocolate is my drug but
I don't know when to stop
So don't tell me that
I can stop having an unhealthy relationship with chocolate

(Now read bottom up)

Re-adjust

We're on a fleeting journey
On a planet green and blue,
Spending time worrying
About what we're meant to do.
We place such pressure
On ourselves and it's too much,
And of life's simplicity
We've become so out of touch.
Rarely focussing on one thing,
We've so much on the go,
No questions left unanswered
There's not a thing that we can't know.
Everything is instantaneous,
Off grid is not a thing,
As we clutch our phones so tightly,
Responding to each ping.
We've rewired our brains
To live in a such a fast-paced way
We think we are experiencing more
As we bolt around each day,
But quality over quantity
Is what I think we need,
And there comes a time in life
To readjust our speed.
So take a breath, look up,
There's so much more to see,
Sometimes be unavailable
It's how we're meant to be.

Hold your tongue

Hold your tongue
It can't be undone…
Things slip out quick,
And the words, they stick.
You can't take them back,
Once things have been said,
They become entrenched
Stuck inside of your head.
Those true micro-thoughts,
That come from the Id,
That are best to let pass
Should have kept on the lid.
Hold your tongue
It can't be undone
This isn't the time to spout,
And let that anger slip out.
Those who shout the loudest
Aren't always struggling more,
And the words can cause damage
Shattering the recipient's core.
Hold your tongue
It can't be undone
The anger will fade,
Don't release the shade.
Reflect for a second,
That you won't regret
Because angry words
They are hard to forget.

Oh, younger self

Oh, younger self,
What advice I'd give to you,
Don't listen to anything
It's probably untrue…
You were old before your time,
You grew up way too fast,
And now you wish you hadn't
But you cannot change the past.
Your friends will come and go,
But the truest ones will stay,
Despite the complications
That life throws in the way.
Enjoy those special moments
Of complete and utter bliss,
Because it's the simple things
That you will really miss.
Don't worry about what others think,
It will stop you feeling whole,
And by the time you hit your twenties,
It will start to take its toll…
Don't compare your path to others,
There's no similarity to find,
Support the ones around you,
It pays off when being kind.
Be honest with your values,
Don't allow them to slide,
And when you're feeling vulnerable
Remember not to hide.

Oh, younger self,
So much advice that I would give,
But in order to be wiser
You must learn it as you live.

Standards

Unapologetically set standards,
That no-one's allowed to lower,
And you will get to where you need
Albeit a little slower.
But worth the wait, for quality,
Expectations will soon thrive,
And relationships worth waiting for
Will soon start to arrive.
Standards must be held calmly,
No preached or yelled or screamed,
And sometimes it's silence needed
For your pride to be redeemed.
Remember that their ceiling,
Can sometimes be your floor,
And that's a problem in itself
That you cannot ignore.
So, change yourself for no one,
Keep holding your head high,
Don't realign your standards
For it's a skill not to comply.

Lost in mind; found at heart

Moments of intense despair,
Desperation and dismay,
The certainty in every bone,
That things won't be okay.
Panic like no other,
Fear, anger and distress,
No ability to see beyond
The suffocating mess.
My mind temporarily gone,
In the chaos, it escaped,
My vision blurred entirely,
All distorted and misshaped.
Yet somehow things do calm,
The havoc starts to fade,
I begin to find myself again,
No longer so afraid.
I remember that inside of me,
There's a heart that beats so strong,
And I can learn to live in peace
Despite when things go wrong.
I release the pain into words,
So that my being can re-start,
Knowing when I'm lost in mind,
I'll be rescued by my heart.